Rege

of with me gr—

me your opposite
number in Connect Ed,
for all of a decade!
Love

Mary
x

CELEBRATION
AFFIRMATION
PROTEST

CELEBRATION
AFFIRMATION
PROTEST

Poems
Charles Eden

Celebration Affirmation Protest
Charles Eden

Published by Greyhound Self-Publishing 2023
Malvern, Worcestershire, United Kingdom.

Printed and bound by Aspect Design
89 Newtown Road, Malvern, Worcs. WR14 1PD
United Kingdom
Tel: 01684 561567
E-mail: allan@aspect-design.net
Website: www.aspect-design.net

ISBN: 978-1-915803-06-1

Contents

Exercise

Heavy with eating and the warmth of the fire
Then heaving himself forth into the unavoidable light
The yard icy and the cold
Tautening slightly his fat soul
He went out and down the field
To where the logs lay.
Fingers fumbled the heavy wedge
And his grip slipped on the smooth haft
Till the hammer struck and the blade bit.
Years of hit and miss had instructed his stance
And the steel sank into the groaning cleft,
At every swing the aim renewed,
Dulling silver facets into iron resistance.
Tang of metal, breath of man, ringing round.

The world sharpened to a duel,
All bluntness to an edge,
Till rough geometry burst the grain
And the clean halves rolled back.

And now the smugness of the well-stocked wood-store.

Meadowsweet

Where cows move udder-deep
Through buttercups and grass
And alders wet their feet
In waters as they pass,

The fume of meadowsweet
Attracts the butterfly
And drowsy summer heat
Enchants my love and I.

Surpassing any book
Are pastures all in flower,
A meadow by a brook
Invites a careless hour.

So here we'll both sit down
With sights and sounds that please
A mile outside the town
Our restless hearts to ease.

And later turning home,
With pollen on your cheek,
In deepening turquoise gloam
There's nothing more I seek.

White

White world
This wind
Spindrift
Eyes slits
Ice needles
Face blast

Brief lull
Deep drifts
Hot head
Stop and rest
Sweat cools
Go on

Go on
Ascend
Legs sink
White world
Clean lines
Arabesques

Flakes whirl
Firm prints
Smooth bank
Snow gives
Thigh deep
Wallow out

Rock lee
Coat stiff
Brief swig
Follow on

Ice scrapes
Hoar frost
Sun shaft
Bright glare
Blue shade
Gone again

Crust breaks
Sink in
Wind slams
Balance lost
Up again

Legs ache
Breath cold
Throat dry
High bowl
Wind chills
Updrafts
Tracks fill

Drifts deep
Flakes stream
Hands cold
Lines pass
Height gained
Head spins

Air light
Eyes stare
Mouth lolls
Sit down
Lean back
Face numb
End of track

Deep snow
Eyes close
Journey's end
Heart's ease

Pulse slows
Core cold
Mind blank
Let go

Circle down
Sink deep
Mind numb
Succumb

Pilgrim

The feet of the faithful
Have beaten this path through the mountains.
Here at the foot of the climb
Stands a shrine decked with jonquil and crocus.
The snows of the pass
Have melted, and right at the top
The hostel stands ready.
The shutters creak open
And it wakes from its torpor of winter
Startling the gloom of six months.
The guardian welcomes the first of the pilgrims
Who are dumping their burdens
At the door and easing their shoulders.
Sharp savoury smells
Start to banish the must of neglect.
A meal and a bed are the simple requirements
And water to wash the sour sweat
The following day they'll begin the descent
To the parched brown lands of the south
And the bones of Diego
Now roofed with cathedral.

Here on the threshold
They'll queue with the others
To touch in his side
The wound in James' effigy,
Polished by penitents,
Then penetrate further

To the source of the mystery.
Under the censer's sweet smoke
A shuffling line mounts the steps
Now their quest to fulfil
At the sepulchre.
A kiss or a touch
Of the cold stone sarcophagus
And their journey's complete.

In the bright square outside
By the stalls selling trinkets
And row upon row of plaster St James
For that niche by the door,
What is it they feel?
A purging maybe of the body,
A purification?
Or merely the pleasure
Of having said "Yes, I will do it"
Now to have done it.
Is it something they found at the end
Or something they carried within them?
Some say you become
The thing that you worship
So maybe it's both.

We who observe
And are puzzled by pilgrims
All know a place
That is special to us.
For many, a hill is a fine aspiration,
Its summit made sacred
By all those who've stood at this point
And searched the horizon,
Weighing the blues of the distance.

Voyage of Discovery

The infant Jonah explores his world,
Keeps pushing out its borders,
Maps it on an elastic grid,
Somehow aware it must allow for
Plenty more first-time events,
Builds a growing picture.
This tiny intellectual
Ravenous for knowledge,
This brand new little body.
Ravenous for sensation,
This tiny thumping heart
Ravenous for love.
This bold adventurer
Already at the masthead
Eager for landfall.

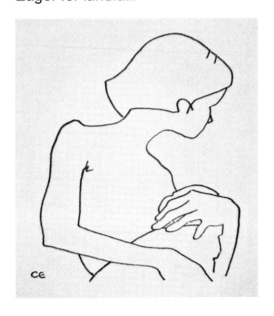

Table

As the altar to the church
So the table to the household.
Here are enacted the secular rituals
And the daily civilities of the family.
Let's leave aside the melamine simulations
And their wipe-clean surface,
And consign to the atrium
That abstraction of polished steel and glass-
The architect's sterile dream.
I have in mind the farmhouse
White scrubbed deal, its raised grain
Now a juddering nuisance
To anyone wishing to write,
Standing four square on kitchen flagstones.
And better still the polished complexities
Of hardwood grain,
These oak boards
A study of art's possibilities,
Of forest's timeless law.
Here are set the fragrant dishes
Of our celebratory meals
But no less important the everyday meals.
Of the ordinary days of our life.

We need this simple ceremonial
Now the vicar's been sent packing
Clutching his bag of tricks,
And now we have to sing our self-penned
Eulogies to mark a passing.

But no, we do not need the fanfare
And the pomp and circumstance-
All that went out with empire.
The Trooping of the Colour
Brightens our grey lives, we're told.
That too will go when crown
Joins cassock and pith helmet
And judge's powdered wig
In the musty dressing-up box of history.

We need a new ceremonial.
Let's start with tables.

Voices

O what do the clouds tell us,
What do the clouds tell us,
Processing across the sky
Like sheets hung up to dry,
Bright and immanent with meaning
Voyaging towards the evening?

And what is it the earth tells us,
What can we read,
Pressed within the pages of its book,
If we should only care to look,
Grasses, trees and creatures of the past?
Lessons that nothing can last,
Nothing can last.

Surely limpid water whispers something clear,
Its sibilant syllables reaching our ear,
As it wends its way seaward
Through stream, pool and weir?
The river an artery to the land
Its movement the pulse in our hand.

Then what can the fire tell us,
What would it name,
With its twin dancing tongues
And its heart of white flame?
I destroy, I create,
Without love, without hate.
Bend me to your will
Or my nature's to kill.

And so sang the wind
And so lisped the water
And so spelled the earth
And so sighed the fire.
If these you hold dear
Revere, revere, revere.

Quest

Scientists with their tables and their grids,
Their rulers and their scales
And their desire to cram the universe
Into a small box,
Their need to reduce and to render down,
Have run god into a corner
And lo! He's just a bloke in a white coat
Like them, with nothing to say.

Down at the feminist workshop
They've pegged him out on a bench,
Busy deconstructing him
-Careful with those shears, ladies-
Now reduced to a mannequin
They're giving him a makeover,
Doing a slap-up job,
Reassembling him in their image.

In the church under the vaulted roof
The congregation rise
At the organ's blast
And sing the familiar words
Extolling the battle, the rugged pathway,
The pilgrimage to the source of light,
The celestial city:
A comfort shawl knitted for them
By generations of the faithful.

The artist's visionary yearning
Has made a fragile enclosure,
An abode where may dwell a deity
Reverenced by acts of creation.
Fathered by need
Mothered by love
And seeking a place
Where one day they might meet
In awed recognition.

Prayer Flag

For the opening of the village green
In light-leaved May
-Its pond, its bench, its dipping platform,
Its massive oak and poplar-
The children made prayer flags.
Say rather they were wishes,
One only for each child,
Or if words failed, a picture
Or a symbol, drawn or daubed,
According to ability and age,
On a rough oblong of cotton
To be strung together in a rope
And tied between the branches
Of the trees around the pool.
Ephemeral hieroglyphics and personal ideograms
Amongst the careful verses in calligraphic hand

Now the vivid colours
Viewed in leafless winter are bleaching
Battered by the seasons'
Rain and sun and wind.
The prayers and wishes broadcast
Around the parish and beyond,
Falling as manna on fields and roofs
And woods and streams.
Finally weathered into potency
They flutter still amongst
The rainy leaves of poplar,
While down below
The carefree village children grow.

Gelato

Somewhere near the sea
A terrace mid-afternoon
And canopied shade
Beneath a fierce sun.
Glare outside,
Soft gloom within.
The tissues at each table
Lifted briefly by the breeze.
And she, bare-shouldered,
Just a hint of burn.
In her sundae glass
Two scoops of strawberry sorbet
Just soft enough to yield.
In her hand for spoon
A small and sharp-edged
Scallop shell,
Delicately lifted
Fingers fanned,.
To her red mouth, pouting.
Briefly eye-beams tangle.
"Yes, you may look again
But please don't stare."
Ah, for pity, signorina,
For beauty of the moment,
Yield.

Cave

Enter with me under these tree roots
On all fours through this ooze
Of liquid silt, till the lintel is passed
And the passage opens low and black
Into the interior of the earth.
From now on all we see is what
The cone of light from our headtorch
Jerks into visibility.
Pitch black pools are passed
Where live blind fish whose skin is white.
From time to time we stop
Where we can stand upright
And gather in a circle
Our faces masks. "Turn off your light",
Someone says. The last one is reluctant.
"Put your hand in front of your face."
Nothing. Darker than any night ever.
Annihilating blackness closes in
Bringing with it silence.
Someone turns their light on
Allowing others to do the same.
We're a long way from the entrance
And think about our route.
The lefts would all be rights
And all the rights be lefts
If we returned this way.
There is some smell. What is it?
What's the smell of rock?

Maybe some mineral seam
Imprisoned aeons ago..
A flat smell of metals, rust perhaps.
And apart from us the only sound
Is water, in which we step
Or which we hear in drips
Dropping from the roof
Whenever we stop.
A silent, black mineral world.

The passage gives out, a ramp descends
To God knows what elaborations.
We're further down. A level way
Leads on through thigh-deep water
Growing slowly less. Knee-deep.
And now we see
A pinpoint in the distance.
Resigned, we toil but soon perceive
Through less resistance
A slow emergence into water
Ankle deep.
The pinprick has enlarged.
And now we see-we see!
That it is light we see
Enlarging slowly
To an exit and return.
First a scent of plants
A glimpse of cumulus edge
White on blue.

And now the sound of distance
And of birdsong
On the moving air.
We emerge re-born
From the innards of the earth,
A voyage of rediscovery
Now happy to be home.

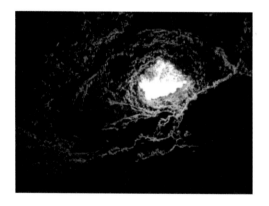

Cookie

Suddenly that dated and dusty
Piece of brown furniture
Started to sing.
It started to sing
Straight to our dusty hearts
When Cookie first sat down,
When he first sat down to play.
And his big broad back,
His bracered back
Bent over the keys,
Was what we looked at
As he shook out showers
Of delicate notes.
Waves and showers of delicate notes.
With shining eyes we looked
When Cookie sat down
On the stool
And from a dead stick
Made green leaves spring,
When Cookie sat down
And made furniture sing.

Home

Home is the place, said Mr Frost,
Where when you go
They have to let you in

The natural habitat of my family
Says Mum,
As a nest for a bird.

A prison, says youth,
With warders checking on you,
A cage to prowl.

A springboard into life,
Says the adventurer,
Then a refuge on my retreat.

Not here, the life to come
Say the faithful,
Where I shall know as I am known.

The place of decent working people
Says the politician,
Suckers one and all for my flattery.

Dear old planet Earth fast receding
Says the astronaut,
Voyaging into lifeless space.

Where your heart is
Croon a thousand schmaltzy songs
Relieving you of your buck.

Where my compass points
Coos the pigeon
Obedient to the imperative of instinct.

The campfire in the middle
Says the gypsy
Whittling a stick under the stars.

A journey of rediscovery
Says the mountaineer
From barren top to green awaiting valley.

White ducks in the yard
Says the refugee
And mother calling us in to bed.

The smell of parsley
Said the drowned sailor,
All I'm left with is the shrivelled word.

Teme River – Wild Daughter of Severn

A litany of loveliness
The names that grace the twisting Teme.
Come climb together from mouth to source,
Twined with paths its silver gleam.

Past Bransford's bridge, the barn at Leigh,
Soughing wind through Lulsley's trees,
Grating of gears up Ankerdine,
Cropping of grass on Ham Bridge leas.

Through Martley's red rock portal
The accompanying road descends,
Entrance to her vale of enchantments,
High banks and fast-flowing bends.

Long, rounded limbs and female forms
Smooth the valley's steep sides,
Under dark dingles of gruesome name,
Where the Severn's Wild Daughter rides.

A Shelsley with a sandstone church,
The other built of travertine,
Clifton above and Stanford athwart
The river on its wandering line.

Mamble – a secret not to tell –
Eastham's wrecked bridge stood here,
Tenbury's annual mistletoe fair
And Clee whose brow shows clear.

Dreaming cows under orchard trees,
Hopyards and fields of ripening wheat:
A surviving mixed farm, unusual now,
Where Hereford, Worcester and Salop meet.

Turning north at Wooferton,
Ashford Bowdler savours fear.
His sister Ashford Carbonel,
Her pretty bridge above the weir.

Ludlow is a fluttering flag
High on its prosperous hill,
While just above lies Bromfield,
Horse chestnut shading water-mill.

Swinging west through Downton Gorge
Past Burrington's headstones of iron
To the parlour pub at Leintwardine,
Then Bucknell and Brampton Bryan.

Knighton and Knucklas, train into Wales,
Llanfair Waterdine, Mary's church,
Beguiling Beguildy beckons us to
The final village in our search.

Felindre turns its ghostly wheel,
We leave behind its last abode
To climb up bare Cilfaesty Hill,
The last we see of house and road.

We ascend to only earth and sky
And leave behind all settlements,
A journey suddenly back through time
To the primordial elements.

The dwindling stream we follow to
A fount that's hidden in a fold,
And here we stand and gaze as if
It were the fabled crock of gold.

Our pilgrimage is now complete
We've traced it to its bubbling spring.
Our presence makes a sacred place
No gifts we've brought, ourselves we bring.

Now bead the names upon a thread
To make a charm to wake a dream,
That litany of lovely names
Found on the peaceful banks of Teme.

The Good-Enough Gardener

"Show me the attendance register
And I will show you the man,"
I once mocked in Churchillian tones
To some deputy head.
"Well, it's true, "she said,
Missing the irony.
And yes, I do remember Bill's register
Was a work of art:
No alterations, no deletions,
Every stroke deliberately made
At a precise angle,
The colours uniform black
And one shade only of red
For absence, indicated always
With a perfect circle.
But then Bill was a maths teacher
And he was my mate
So I forgave him, despite coming
A very poor second to him
With the Attendance Officer

So now I repeat to all
You middle managers out there,
Guardians of the holy flame:
"Show me the garden
And I will show you the man."

Bill, I'm afraid your register,
Horticulturally viewed,
Is that severe square of grass
Bordered by strict lines
Of red soldier tulips
Standing to attention after
Drilling on the parade ground
Of the suburban front garden.

And even Gardeners' Question Time-
See, I do take an interest-
Harboured once a Dr Stefan Buczacki
Of the fascist tendency
Who described a weed thus:
"Any plant growing in the wrong place."

And indeed Gardeners' Tendency-
Sorry, Question Time-
Despite its warm-hearted tolerance
Of backsliders,
Always has ready in the shed,
If the occasion demands,
The appropriate proprietary poison
To exterminate, exterminate.

It is not that I choose to make
My garden a sanctuary for weeds
But that they flee
The persecution of my neighbour
And apply for political asylum
And I haven't the heart
To send them back.

And at Guarlford Nursery
Carol looked a little crestfallen
When I announced I was disappointed
That I had sought in vain for a plant
With a label that said
"Thrives on neglect."
Graciously (gardening makes you gracious)
She said, "What you mean
Is one that will grow anywhere."

Gardens have little time
For the truly indolent
And have a way of letting
You, and everyone, know.
Nevertheless I have no regrets,
Well, not many anyway,
That thirty years ago in the middle
Of forking the veg patch
A heavenly searchlight picked me out
And the voice of the sage was heard
And it spake unto me thus:
"Thou coulds't be doing this

In thy dotage."
Whereupon I took the fork
And drave it into the mould
And left it quivering with shock
And walked away, never,
Well, hardly ever, to return.

But many's the time since then
That I've felt the power of the earth:
When Geoff took a handful of soil
Rich in humus and said
"Look at that. Put that in your pipe
You could smoke it." Or Ray
When he took some soil in his hand
And compressed it and felt it
Spring back in his fist.

So now I invite you into my garden
With its very mixed borders
Of flowers and weeds,
And even a plot of hesitant veg,
In the hope-no, not hope, expectation
That you will smile graciously
On my weak endeavours
And with me agree
That a man is revealed by his garden,
His vulnerability all on display.

Skip

See the skip upon the pavement
Filling up with last year's stuff.
Out with the old, in with the new,
Never say enough's enough

Life is change and life is movement,
Once aboard you cannot stop,
Skim the catalogue, thumb the brochure,
Shop until you nearly drop.

Anyway, the economy needs it,
Business wants us all to spend.
Got no money? Don't you worry,
Bury your head, the banks'll lend.

………………………………………

That was then, but now we realise
That a day of reckoning comes
For a person, for a country,
That refused to do its sums.

The bankers and their chums are laughing
That we thought they'd give a fuck
About the hole they've pushed us into
Where for years and years we're stuck.

Caring capitalism? My arse!
Know the nature of the beast:
The world must toil and all its children
So a few fat cats can feast.

Cold wind's blowing from the future.
Only way when greed is rife
Is to reinvent community,
Look for each other, value life.

Keep the pure flame bright and burning
Source of warmth and source of light,
Work together for tomorrow,
Urge the dawn that follows night.

Goodbye Dubai

I met a traveller from a distant land
Who told me of a city on a sea,
Built by the grateful poor of all the world,
Whose lofty towers in proud ascendancy
Bore witness to that restless power of man
To twist the laws of nature to his end,
Displace the water, cast away the sand,
And so construct-not personally, of course-
An artificial Megalopolis,
Apt shrine to visit money's golden source.

Since then the rumour spreads from shore to shore
The folly's fallen, insects mine the floor.
The lesson's very clear: to all I roar
"Show Mammon and his cohorts out the door!"

Upton Carnival

A happy accident in Upton upon Severn:
When finally the wraps were removed
The new bridge shimmered
In tropical colours,
A gaudy macaw screeching delightedly
In its new Brazilian strip.

Oh, Dr Socrates, you must have conjured this,
Your last glorious trick,
Twinning neat little Upton
With Rio at carnival time.

A gorgeous goal right out of the blue
That makes the sun smile.
So Upton heralds the World Cup
And the Olympics, joins the BRICs.

Yes, the painters got it wrong
But now we know they dipped
Their brushes in joyful serendipity,
Challenged the townsfolk to forget
Their careful ballot and accept
This happy visitation,
Their own new tethered rainbow.

Work

If work is to really engage us,
I remember the potter once said,
It should satisfy all of our nature,
Our heart, our hand and our head.

He spoke, as he gave his attention
To creating a pot on his wheel,
The wet grey slip oozing out of his hands
As he drew up its shape by its feel.

The celestial potter blew life into us.
We're told ,at the dawning of day,
And for our first test he plonked us in Eden,
Said "Have fun," then he went on his way.

For a year, maybe two, it was heaven
Just strolling about in the buff,
With his eyes on her and her eyes on his
They thought they could never get enough.

But there's always a snag with things human
-You're thinking the snake and our fall-
You're right, but what really got to them,
The pleasures had started to pall.

A big creamy cake it is naughty but nice,
If you're offered you'll maybe have two,
But if you try to eat seven or eight
There's a fair chance you're going to spew.

And so it befell with our Jack and Jill
-Better say Adam and Eve-
"Please not ambrosia and nectar again,
Just hearing the names makes me heave."

So finally, when they are told to depart
And sweat daily for water and bread,
A small inner voice said "He's probably right"
As out from the park they both fled.

And so it has been since eviction
That we've lived by the sweat of our brow
-Or should, but division of labour
Meant that most had to follow the plough.

While others just dished out the orders
They'd had dished to them by the squire,.
Who spent his day counting his money
While the hard-handed labourers expired.

If you're wondering where all this is leading
It's to redefine work that I strive.
Keep the work-life balance? Not likely
When we're yours from eight until five.

When we work all the day for the evening,
For the weekend we work and we wait,
And the weeks we must save for vacations,
But we're back in there Monday at eight.

When we save up our years for retirement,
When we leave all the living on hold
In the hope that some day in the future
It'll all be repaid seven-fold.

To return to verse one and the potter
-You remember his heart ,head and hand-
If you want proper job satisfaction
You'll get nowhere until you demand

That life must go on in the workplace,
Not be treated as something discrete:
For work to be truly worth doing
There're vital criteria to meet.

Not a robot on the assembly line,
Nor computer in front of a screen,
For these are both forms of enslavement
That turn people into machines

If we only do what's life-enhancing
We'd get rid of the jobs that waste time,
And production of unneeded items
Would be clearly revealed as a crime.

So do it for love of the doing
And think it for love of the thought
And feel it for common humanity
This way only our souls can't be bought.

Birthday Blues

Woke up this mornin'
        Couldn't quite locate the pain.
Woke up this mornin'
        Say I couldn't locate the pain.
Suddenly I realise-yes,
        It's my goddam birthday again

Folks give you presents
        Don't know what they're doin' to me,
Family take your picture
        Wish that they would let me be.
Yes, I know it sounds ungrateful
        Not to celebrate your anniversary.

Every year it happens
        Matter what you do or say,
Yes, every year it happens
        Even if with gold you try to pay
That ol' gypsy man Time
        To stop his wagon rollin' and stay.

Wanna press the ol' pause button
        Enjoy a year or two of now,
Press that crazy button
        Ain't quite figured how
Make the present stay the present jus' for now.

Society out in Paris
    Demonstrates against New Year,
Call themselves SOCONA
    Wish they had a section here.
March down Champs Elysees
    When the midnight hour is near.

Only kinda present
    I would really like to use
Is this lil' harmonica
    To play the birthday blues.
Yes, I know you can't escape it-
    Jus' don't wanna pay my dues.

National Treasure

Admit first to the pantheon David Attenborough
Who for most of our lives
Has offered our planet for inspection,
Monochrome and colour,
His words and the warmth of his voice
And his wonder still bright.
Simply presenting the facts
For us to decide,
Has made us custodians
And stewards of creation,
Has alerted us lately
That it could be last post
For the greens and blues of this world.

Next, to my republican astonishment, the Queen.
Yes, like her swans, paddling hard
Underwater to maintain the illusion
Of calm, to keep that dated vessel
On an even keel, unhelped by her crew,
Whilst looking serenely in control
On the bridge.
But to see the little lady
In Ireland confronting God knows what,
Outfacing implacable foes,
Sincerity neutralising the acids
Of hatred and fear,
Offering a hurt people the hand of friendship,
Not knowing if it will be spurned,
And winning the admiration of most
Including, to my surprise, me.

And while he's still with us, Ken Dodd,
The idiot-savant of Knotty Ash,
His remaining hair charged by
The ten thousand jokes just below
Racing round in his circuitry.
He doesn't know when to stop, you know.
Or is it that they won't let him go?
The line of coach drivers outside
Look at their watches and sigh
As faintly some hear the uproar within.
"I don't know what you're laffin at, missus.
Was it something I said?"

Victoria Wood is another with this genius
For assuming a voice and a character
-a special British trait.
Humanising everything she touches
She celebrates us: dinner ladies,
Lollipop ladies, usherettes and weekend ramblers.
Yuh know, ordinary folk.
She's everyone's clever aunty playing the piano
And singing cheeky songs in the front room,
Her extraordinary talent
Harnessed to the talent of ordinary folk.
Oh, Ms Wood, just beat me, beat me,
Beat me on the bottom with the Woman's Weekly.

Next skip up Ramona Marquez.
Who? says you.
You know, the little girl in Outnumbered
AKA Karen Brockman, now aged ten,
The terrible enfant sage
Whose fierce honesty has her parents
Game, set and match,
Her Dad struck thoughtful and silent
By her "But you said…"
And her Mum wondering again
How she gave birth to this wonder.
A vulnerable child when all's said and done,
Still desperately needing their love
OK, a fiction, I know, but fiction
That's facter than fact.

Lastly step up Gareth Malone
From whatever realms of glory
You've miraculously emerged
To breeze in and convince us
That we can do it.
To bring back the turned-away,
To get the doubtful lads
From down the gym to take
Their barber shop act around the pubs.
To show us again and again
That we only need encouragement,
Direction and encouragement,
To bump along to take-off
And the sudden realisation
That we're off the ground
And now in tremulous flight
And that our pilot has gone
And is now far below, waving
With confident astonishment
That we are airborne
And flying aloft on our own.

Scav

Invertebrates lack backbone you know
Small wonder they prop up the heap,
The base of a virtuous triangle
Where their nature fates them to creep.

Above this order stalk reptiles, fly raptors,
Proof of the principle of life:
Might always right and eat or be eaten,
The animal ethic of strife.

Humanity of course transcends all of this,
Liberty, equality, so on.
The law of the jungle? Surely not us
With our model of God's only son.

You'll remember how Maggie once phrased it,
To wait for the trickle-down effect.
Well they waited and waited and waited
And now of course they suspect

That Maggie and Dave, even Tony,
Are there to look after the rich
And the best they can offer the rest of us
Is just a politico's pitch.

So rise up you ants and you beetles
You've nothing to lose but your head,
You'll inherit the world in the sweet by and by
Once Dave, and humanity's, dead.

Motel Eldorado

We open first the door into our room
Turn on the light. OK. What you'd expect.
Go get our bag and swing it on the rack
Then flop down zonked upon the double bed
Grateful to stop at last at this motel
Somewhere between our start and our arrival.

The usual services tidily arranged
Only a greasy smudge where headboard
Ought to be tells us we are not the first
To spend the night in this white box
Beside the roaring highway.

Tele jabbers. Shower hisses. Gradually
The fizz subsides and heaviness now comes.
Events of the day twitch behind our eyes
Or play upon the white screen of the wall,
The non-stop roar outside now muted.

Remnants of the day dance still in our heads
In the settled landscape of dream memory.

Jolted awake in the death hour. Where am I?
In the silence only the doppler crescendo
Diminuendo of the comings and
Goings of occasional lorries
The ceiling now stroked by the lighthouse sweep
Of their beam.

We awake to bright light through the curtains,
The roar of the road continuous already,
Early checkouts now a hundred miles
Down the highway. A coffee and doughnut
And we hurry to join them.

Maria arrives in her flip-flops
And shift, pushing a trolley, chewing on gum.
She changes bed linen and towels to take
To the laundry before the cleaners begin.
Used to detritus, not shocked by people
When she opens the door and lets in the morning.

Sometimes she finds some cash on the table
And dreams of the journey back south
On the highway, the road that she first travelled north
To the golden pavements of promise.

She picks up the coins and thinks of her children,
Pulls locked the door and moves onto the next.

Nets

For the fisherman always the focus
Is the catch. Hard hands haul on the hempen
Ropes as they draw in the nets from the deep.
All that extensive cordage enclosing
Something-or nothing-caught in the centre,
The circle tightening and drawing in.
Then the emergence of the rounded load
Of the catch suspended, the shedding of
Water, glitter of water cascading
And the dump and release on the deck.

Now the thump and slither of rubbery bodies
Subsiding from thrashing to twitching.
The surf of the boat down the wave
And the spindrift sharp in our face.
The wallow, the welter, the flash of the knives,
Overalls and boots now sequined with scales
And the plunge of the gulls for the guts
In the tumult and heave of the sea.

In the house on the bay now lighted
Against the dark, hands smooth the sheet,
Touch fevered cheek in the child's room.
Blent with soft words, healing sleep
Soon returns quiet breath.
And then in the room below
Hands resume careful work,
Threads of silk lend their colour
To the design.

Heart, head and hand together
Embody a vision held in the mind.
Days, even weeks must pass
Until this patient craft
Moves to completion.

Outside across the bay
A lighted boat passes.

Weave between them a net
Steel of silk in the warp
Cord of hemp in the weft.
Hard hand of fisherman
Soft hand of wife
Weaving together
The threads of their life.

The Fourth Plinth

An empty plinth's a potent vacancy
And once invited many fools emerge
To fill the void, but mostly with themselves-
Vanity ever was a powerful urge.
Antony Gormley compered the first show,
Who puts his likeness everywhere he can.
His rigid, lifeless statues stare ahead
Though some would have it that they stand for
Man.

The panel's met and now the choice is made:
A monstrous crowing cock in brightest blue
Will lease the plinth a year, and then a boy
Astride a rocking horse for one year too.

And so what figure merits permanence,
What symbol's potent in this London square?
Enclosed with gallery, church and embassy,
In this arena what idea should dare?

Onto the empty plinth behind Power's back
An anonymous figure now ascends,
No noble gaze, no jutting chin, but one
On whom a true democracy depends.

The figure could be any one of us
Who looked and saw and said "This isn't right."
So if not now then when and if not me
Then who will drag the matter up into the light?

The health of a democracy is known
By how its whistleblowers are treated.
Most lose their jobs, are ridiculed or worse,
On some the final punishment is meted.

Instead, beyond belief, what is proposed
A sanctified Margaret Thatcher there installed.
Champion of individual greed,
Scorner of fellow feeling. Be appalled.

Dark and Light

Yes, I remember the gravelly-voiced
Northern MP delivering his speech
Solid in the certainties of the struggle
Master against Man. And I looking on

Envied the simple polarities
That resolved the mess like iron filings
Drawn to north or south. And iron I thought
Was in that voice who for years had endured

The battering noise of the factory floor
That wanted him only for speed and skill
Of his hand : not his soul beaten to a thou
By the heavy hammer of his work.

Down there in the boom of the bins filling up
And the squeal of machines, the air full of
Hot oils and the earth smell of metals
And curls of swarf making springs underfoot.

Who would not applaud the steady advance
Of the robots, progeny of these machines,
Making redundant the toils of the past-
But mocking the pride labour took in its work.

So it must have been for cartographers
Mapping a flat earth centuries ago,
All that ingenuity misplaced
All that energy misdirected.

So it was for quarries of millstones,
Their final efforts still lying where left
Under the gritstone edges of Derbyshire
When the foreman called
"Leave those few, lads. We'll have to come back."
But back they never came. Never, ever came.

And I on the night shift at Lucas
Assembling starter motors on the line.
Some of them had been doing it for years
The damage invisible, just the odd tic.

Parts would clatter down metal chutes
Into bins, the shriek of drills
And the bang of the press
A constant backdrop.

It's said if you listen to an alpine herd
Each with its own tonking bell
That you can pull out any tune that you want
Amidst the random notes, haphazard movements.

And I have noticed when mountaineering
How mist and snow, fatigue and night
At the end of a fraught and lengthy day
Can make the mind frantic for meaning
Having nothing to make sense of,

Hearing voices in wind and water,
Seeing apparitions in mist
And light where light doesn't exist.
When the mind drags its anchor
Euphoria and alarm contend.

And so it was on the night shift.
Incessant noises pounded the brain
Until one night I heard, I thought

A station announcement. No this cannot be.
I stepped back and listened.
Even more distinct: "The train arriving
On platform four…" Whoa, time to go.

Birmingham then was the city
Of a thousand trades.
Don't like it?Jack it in.
Find another one tomorrow.

But you can't stop progress, can you.
Can you? And thing's have moved on.
A fine and honourable tradition
The fight for our rights
Now airbrushed out of the history books
Unless we're alert.

The certainties now have been blurred,
A dark and a light mixed into grey
Where all is indistinct.
And I am nostalgic for past certainties
When the ogre overshadowed us with his club,
When the common cause was joined.
Against the common enemy.

But now all-devouring Mammon
And his sweet-talking agents
Infect all of our lives
And try to convince us
It's all for our good

We need a new contract..
Let's rip up the old one
And let's start again.

His Story

Once upon a time, children,
One hundred years ago
There was a very bloody war-
Great-great granddad had to go.

Be over in six months, they said,
Go out and do your best
For King and country, then return,
A medal on your chest.

We went in droves, few came back whole,
What happened in between-
The murder of the innocents
By the military machine.

I mean both sides. The enemy
Were closer to my friends
Than the fools who gave the orders
And sealed our mutual ends.

When it was finally over
In village, town and city
Names on a peace memorial
Were recalled in pity.

Now the centenary arrives
Surely they wouldn't try
To make it a celebration
Of national victory.

A proper commemoration
For those who gave their life
Would require a resolution:
Non-violent resolution of strife.

Great-great grandchild, I wish for you
A better world than mine
Where nations renounce state violence
And we celebrate mankind.

Spem in Alium

"Carlow? Why go to Carlow? There's nothing there,"
Asked Nellie Brennan, nearly ninety now,
Who's happily spent the whole of her long life
About the fields and farmhouse of A Clare.

Mind you, she'd never been to Dublin-
Two hours on the train- until last year.
"I've everything I want right here," who
Barefoot went to school in this same valley.
,
Closed in by Saddleback and Brandon Mountain
Its pilgrim cross against the sky,
And east, the dark wall of the Blackstairs.
But Carlow on the River Barrow, sorry Nellie,

Boasts a grand Arts Centre. And on the day
We went the vast white hall was empty but
For forty stands and speakers in a circle
Playing Thomas Tallis's "Spem in Alium."

Soprano, Alto, Tenor, Baritone and Bass:
Five voices in each choir, eight of these choirs,
In all forty voices, a speaker given to each
So it was possible to listen to
Each separate voice by circling round.

This is the music that Clive Stafford Smith,
British lawyer, defending capital offenders,
Must play each night he's back in his hotel
After battling red-neck jurors all the day,

To purge his affronted soul, to restore
Some sense of other world, some cleaner place
Called up by this exquisite music
So that tomorrow he can start anew.

Forty voices journeying separately
Each unaware of others till at last
All are suddenly blent in harmony
And surge together upward, fill the hall.

Outside the auditorium, at the desk,
Someone has written in the Visitors' Book
It was for them a day trip to paradise.
They're right, it's nothing less, a moment out of time.

Back at A Clare Nellie seeks reassurance
That all this business of the catholic priests
Should still permit retention of a simple faith.
What can you say?
The church is one thing: faith's of a different order.

But now especially, feeling once again
The silent detonation of these spring days,
Then Nellie might book and keep safe in her purse
A single ticket to Carlow, to Dublin, to Paradise.

The Genuine Sort

Our frustrated coach driver
Having been checked by a piece
Of car-driving idiocy
In Sidbury near the cathedral,
Turned his head slightly
And out of the corner of his mouth
To no-one in particular, said
"I don't know where they finds 'em
But when they does
They always sticks one in Worcester."

I think our driver was the genuine sort,
As Willy Carson says of horses
-Not all of them, by any means-
Circling in the parade ring.

But if you wish to admire the human equivalent
in its natural habitat, go no further
than the Market Square in Ledbury
and from your perch in the Market Café
watch them circling for your inspection
oblivious of your gaze, homo sapiens rough-hewn
and in their home environment,
all lumps and bumps
and ever so slightly oddly dressed,
headgear and footgear a study in themselves
but definitely, all too definitely, human.

And when you've gazed your fill
To the point of voyeuristic smugness
You are aware that someone now
Is staring in at you and realise
It's your own reflection in the window
And only hope that you too
Would be thought
The genuine sort.

Going Home

Drawn by what lodestone, I return again,
Obedient to the pull of childhood's power,
To search these bleak remains of neighbourhood
Whose cold back for welcome's all I get,
The road where I grew up now bulldozed,
Its name-notorious- even that has gone.

The place I seek lies whole somewhere within, Too
deeply mapped to fade, its contours
Still the same and demarcated still by watchtower
spire
And distant dome. Its farthest limit
The far-off hill and single tree against
The sky, that called me then as now.

Strange satisfaction here to witness
All this change time's wrought in it and me,
Its mean streets largely gone. But suddenly
Intact amidst the ruins the old school stands
Miraculously spared, and children still
Oblivious to the Old Boy passing by.

Here ancient dames, long gone, did for us all
With their National Folk Song, country dancing,
Poetry and illustrated stories-
Pretty girls on tiptoe watching flying
Clouds, that filled us full of yearning,
Impossible in the greyness of post-war.

I feel once more the warmth of Mother's hand
Leading us daily through an impoverished land.
And now I must get used until the end
To a new cold hand that wants me for a friend.

Father

Father, rarely Dad,
Is looking over my shoulder.
I hear his "humph"
As he reads these lines
And recognises
My reservations.

A disappointment to him
And I not concerned enough
To try very hard
To make it different.
A stranger to me really,
Always at work.

So a mother's son,
Further reason for his scorn,
Essential message
Reduced to slogans
"It's a hard life, Charles."
"If you're not the hammer, you're the anvil."

In recollection
Small islands of warmth
Including here in Ledbury
At the museum in Church Lane-
A mock-up Edwardian classroom,
Poem written on the blackboard.

Coming out again I felt from behind
A tug on my jacket
And turned to see my Dad
Oratorical forefinger raised,
Oblivious and reciting
Masefield's "Sea Fever."

"I must go down to the seas again,
To the lonely sea and the sky
And all I ask is a tall ship
And a star to steer her by…"

This boy who remembered it
From school in Aberdeen
Which he left at fourteen
To help his uncle on his fish –round,
This boy abandoned by his parents
And coming south for work

Where he met my mother
Who saved him from the Spanish civil war.
The rest is history, my history,
In turn abandoning us
For Brazil of all places
To find his fortune

Where such eventually
Was the regard they had
That he was made a Free Man
Of the city of Campinas
Where now he lies buried.

"And quiet sleep and a sweet dream
When the long trick's over."

Moor Pool. Harborne, Birmingham
                    – my mother's birthplace

Fired by their Christian beliefs and vision
Of the good life, industrialists of
The later nineteenth century designed
Communities, projections of their love,

For their workforce and their families.
George Cadbury, Quaker, was such a one,
His Bournville and its generous houses
Rebuking capitalist landlords and their slums.

John Nettlefold, a manufacturer,
Designed the pretty suburb of Moor Pool.
"Impossibly utopian", they sneered,
But go there still and see this hidden jewel.

Wide verges, gardens, allotments, spinneys,
Variety of design, clean air and light,
Traditional annual celebrations,
All carefully arranged for our delight.

Its tennis clubs, its pool, its well-built homes
And at its centre thriving village hall
From which radiate its graceful curving roads,
Charm the eye and win the praise of all.

Paternalism? Yes, but wealth well-used.
Since then no doubt, with so much clearer need
Moor Pool's the pattern? Tragically no.
Vision is lost, our lives now ruled by greed.

The shortest love poem in the language
with quite possibly the longest title.

Shuttered room
Mid-afternoon –
Erotic gloom.

Head v Heart

Major Mind barked "Pull yourself together!"
Heart replied "Whatever."

Mid-morning Lull

A mother pushing a pram
Begins to descend the road.
Before her the green canvas shelter
Of a navvies' work site.
Clang of a dropped shovel.
A red-hot brazier hums
And a kettle of pitch
Wafts its sinus-clearing tars.
Spits domesticate the threshold.
Enamelled mugs
Decorate perches.

Mother negotiates the narrows
Avoiding their leers.
A lump of coke squeals under one tyre
Marking the slab.

Heat warps the blue air.

Please Miss, Don't Go

-me sister in Year 8 give me this
to give you miss

Please miss, don't go
Me sister says you're the best
She thinks school's crap
An I do too - sometimes
An you must need a rest
But – you know, please don't go.

She told us ow
You took em down town
To ave coffee in Costas
An not bring each other down
An learn to be ladylike
Like you are miss.

Julie sez to me
You wanna get in er class
Play up a bit, gerra reputation
For bein a bad ass
Cuz for some reason she don't mind
Avin the naughties like us.

Anyway the posh kids like er,
Basically everybody does
She treats us jus the same
She asn't got favourites

Asn't Stephanie – that's er name –
Like some teachers as.

She ain't gonna say so 'erself
But I know she's upset
About you goin. She says
You're a girly-girl oo likes to wear pink
But you're a bloody good teacher
Cuz you've really made er think.

I've never writ so much in me life
So I won't go on any more.
You've always listened to kids like us
So walk back in that door.
I want you to teach ME inYear 10
If you don't there's gonna be war.

Tracey Smith
Year 8 XX

E-Shop

Let your fingers do the walking
Buy it all online,
White van man is on his way
He just needs you to sign.

Your personal profile's known to us
And all your purchasing patterns,
We've got your demographics
Which help our company fatten.

We know your social network
We've narrowed down your choice,
Apart from impulse buys we allow,
Those words in your head are our voice.

We're only the public interface,
Californian geeks are to blame
Who are creaming off the billions,
Playing the world like a game.

Yes, go back to your High Street
To its sale boards and empty shops
But you know it's only a matter of time
Before the penny drops.

We've got you where we want you,
You'll do as you are told
And kid yourself that it's your choice
Since your rights to Mammon you've sold.

Black Country

Sandwell making merry on its gala day
And offering its six towns challenge walk,
Twenty six miles tracing some only
Of its bewildering canal towpaths.

Room too for roads and railways
Clambering over each other, so that
Aqueducts carry canals over canals,
Railway viaducts reach over both
And more recent motorways span the lot
On massive concrete legs.
Natural habitat it seems for
Pylons and ugly metal fencing
Enclosing yards and their forgotten corners.

Along the cut
Towers of pallets balance their random architecture
Against the sky, and a single wall remains
Of some forgotten industry
Awaiting final demolition,
Ghost of former purpose lingering still
And buddleia that thrives on desolation.

Residues of neighbourliness survive,
Product of the solidarity
Engendered by the heavy industry,
The thirty foot seam of coal

And the iron smelters-
Black by day and red by night-
That granddad and his missus
Gave their lives to.

Industrial archaeology still stands
Next to modern oblong warehouse units
That seek to fill the void,
And buried out of sight is Dudley's
Nile pyramid conundrum,
Netherton Tunnel, three thousand and fifty yards
Of arching brickwork built by
God knows who at God knows what expense
Of money, time and men.

Halfway through a shy graffiti artist,
Working in the dark,
Has sought a brief transcendence.
And indeed what better employment
Offers itself, if you are unemployed,
On some wet afternoon
Than a virgin wall beneath a bridge
To vent your powerlessness,
Affirm at least your name-
As has Tojo the Dwarf across one span
While another is memorial to a mate now gone.

Humbled and impressed I now return
To Sandwell showground
And feel within me pushing for
Expression the voice of a people,
Dirt in their DNA, iron in their soul.

Light

I see! breathes the blind man,
The bandages removed.

There! That does it now, complete.
The artist's final brushstroke.

Explosive flash of white-
The martyr's ecstasy.

"Our vision going forward"-
The corporate chairman's drone.

Wah! Shrieks the new-born
Invaded by the common light.

Daily miracles for Blake-
Every thing and every one.

A rediscovered Eden,
Samuel Palmer's Kentish garden.

Random epiphanies
May fall on anyone.

Midshires Farmers

All right, are yer?
Aar.
You still out at Clodbury?
Aar.
Wo chafter today?
Foive undredweight o' Growmore.
You got the trailer with yer?
Aar.
Oy'll ave it put on.

Yafter anything else?
Aar. The missus run short of undies.
Wo chafter? Top or bottom?
Bottom.
What size? Er's a big girl, enner?
Aar.
What kind yafter?
Watcha got?
Standard, fancy or basic.
Standard'll do.

So, large standard. An ow many yafter?
Ow d'they come?
Bale, alf bale, quarter bale.
Oy'll tek alf bale.
So alf bale large standard.
On the trailer?
Aar.

You wan anythin else?

You got any cowcake?
You doin dairy now then?
No.Er likes something to nibble of an evenin
when er's watchin telly.
Ow much yafter?
Er guz through it fast. Oy'll tek a case.
On the trailer?
Aar.

Anythin else?
Nar.
Oy'll be seein you then. Tarra.
Tarra.

Bad Luck, Tracy!

It's awfully bad luck on poor Tracy
She was born in the wrong social class
In a flat on the seventeenth storey-
If you peer you can just see some grass
.

Who knows, with vocational training
Beginning as soon as she can (say age five)
She might find some worthwhile employment,
I'd make that your number one plan.

Something better? Now be realistic
The moment the panel hear her voice
Ninety per cent of life chances
Shut down. Sorry to narrow the choice.

No need to get nasty, get real,
We've paid for our own flying starts,
Wealth must confer some privilege-
Ignore all those sad bleeding hearts.

You thought in the 60's that merit
Had squeezed between money and birth
To offer its crucial life chances
As the paramount measure of worth.

Well it did for a while, or seemed to,
But deep structures stayed safely in place.
So that's about all I can tell you.
Er, good luck in the future, young Trace.

Midwinter, Orkney

The burial chamber at Maes Howe
Within a circular ditch
Carefully sited and aligned

Its low stone passage –blocks of perfect fit-
Must be crawled to the central room
And its three separate vaults.

Midwinter alone if sky is clear
Solstice gold dazzles the back wall
Light of life for chiefs herein interred
With amulets and offerings.

Four thousand years later Vikings invaded
Who engraved the walls with their graffiti.

"Ingibiorg is the finest girl in the north"
And "Many a proud lady, low-stooping,
Has entered here"
As we do too, drawn into the ritual.

Seven Ages of Woman

First the infant gurgling and gurning in her mother's arms
And then the eager schoolgirl with shining morning face
        skipping blithely to school
And then the lover sighing blissfully
        at the sudden intensity of life
        excited by her awakened femininity
Next the young mother juggling family and job
        and their complementary satisfactions
Slow but sure the fulfilment of mature years
        sought out for her wise advice
The sixth age a seated lady watching the world go by
        reflecting on the richness of her days
Last scene of all a mild spring breath lifts the gauze curtain
        On the seasons she'll no longer see.

Bus Club, Wester Ross

Feet broken in by new boots
During severe winter weather
Among Torridon's primeval mountains
I dropped out on the fourth day
And boarded the supermarket bus
From Gairloch to Dingwall
Over a hundred miles return.

Pleasant drone of engine as we climbed
Up past Glen Docherty's woods
Then over open moorlands.
But somewhere near to Achnasheen
A solitary figure stood.
We pulled up and a redhead
Came busily on board.

Hello Brian. How are the bairns?
She called out to our driver
Then joined the talk and what
I realised was their regular club.
We moved through empty landscape
And alongside wild lochs
With only the railway line nearby

At Garve some conversation
Touched upon the recent accident
That had closed both road and rail.
Yes, a young man. Overtaking, they say.
Dead. His car across the line.

Talk then wandered back
To the inconsequential,
The way it will, the way it has to,
This face to face and voice to voice exchange
The soil that sustains community.

Past Strathpeffer, its wild cats
And its Museum of Childhood
To arrive prosaically
In supermarket car park.
The bus would leave in just two hours
So they to do their weekly shop
And I to find the swimming pool.

At one I joined the laden shoppers
Clambering back on board
Telling of bargains and encounters,
But animation slowly fading
As the sun warmed up our left
And we dozed through engine drone
The ups now downs and downs now ups.

The bus routinely stopped
Outside the Kinlochewe Hotel
Where I thanked our driver
And called a general farewell.

Next morning waking to the mantra
That had churned all through my dreams
How are the bairns now, Brian.
Hello Brian. How are the bairns?

Gentle Girl

I write this with a pencil, gentle girl,
One I'm sure you used to do your sketches.

Everywhere I looked for you and then
Happened upon this valley once again,
The one we travelled twice in celebration,
Its empty twisting lanes and pretty meadows,
Its wooded ridges, long mothering limbs
Enfolding and sheltering its fertile fields.

But this is Earth not Eden and high woods
Conceal their dark and worrying dingles,
Devil's Den and Hell Hole, even Death itself
That no one can escape, my darling girl.

Till I might join you I must content myself
With this blessed valley and its lovely
Feminine contours trying to console me
But when you died a half of me died too.

Rust and Chalk

Three sentinel pines above the Teme,
Two outrageously picturesque
Near Shelsley Kings and Stanford,
Atop their symmetrical tumps,
Their grassy knolls; and the third skylined,
A lone pine hanging above Ham Bridge,
Three enfolding this sheltered valley.

Landscape first formed by the shaping forces
And the later sculptings of ice,
Fashioning and smoothing she- shapes,
These trees a triangulation of beauty,
And cradling somewhere within
A corrugated iron barn,.
Neglect carefully tending
Its vivid oxidation.

There on its sunniest wall
I want to write these verses,
Blue chalk against the orange rust
And above the secret river.

There is no Planet B

Look at Greta's frank and fearless eyes
Focused on the future
Above the busy clamour
Of our political masters,
Who are not ashamed because
They're shameless: careful judges of
Exactly where their interest lies.

No Paul, you got it badly wrong
However much we like to quote
When I was a child, I spake as a child,
I thought as a child.
It is the so-called adults
Who see through a glass darkly,
The glass of distortion,
Wilful or imposed.

And it is the child,
Before any grubby deals
Are struck with expedience,
Who sees it clearly as it is,
The emperor's nakedness ,
And uniquely dares to tell us
As has Greta Thunberg,
All touched, some burned by her intense light,
Her generation inspired and fired to action
By a little girl.

Oxford Junior Dictionary revisited

Goblin and elf have been removed
But so have both saint and sin
And indeed the pew and the altar
And carols echoing.

The trilling lark has not been spared,
Raven and starling are gone,
And with them magpie and heron,
Goldfinch and fast-flitting wren.

But surely not the kingfisher,
Turquoise dart rarely seen.
The brook it haunted, its minnows,
Have also been swept down the stream.

The fern's had to go, hillside heather,
The bramble and also the gorse
And with them the stoat and the weasel,
Conkers, blackberries, acorns.

Sinewy blacksmith now banished,
His colt can't be in the pasture,
Along with nectar and buttercup
And the rarely sighted adder.

No rhubarb in the allotment-no allotment-
Where spinach and mint cannot grow,
No lavender, no gooseberries,
No chestnuts and no sycamore.

No piglet outside, no porridge,
And now the vine can't be found.
Instead attachment, celebrity,
Bullet point, blog and broadband.

Only just returned, otter's now gone
And beaver is one of their cull,
Holly and ivy cannot be seen
And no mistletoe hangs in the hall.

Spring it seems is still with us-just
But now without pansy and crocus,
Violet, primrose and bluebell,
Dandelion, poppy and cowslip.

They're only removing redundant birds
And replacing a few wild flowers.
You can talk to your phone, look at your screen.

A desolate future lours.

New Year

I resolve to hold onto these corners,
Only four of them, if it were so neat,
But a geometry of thought and action
To guide me through these poisonous times.

First to uphold the civil servant,
Honorific title we bestow
On those who give their working lives
To serving civic values-not commercial-
The ones that bind us into something bigger,
Yes, society, however much maligned:
Youth workers, teachers, nurses and librarians,
Probation officers and lollipop ladies.

Next I will continue to decry
All of the forces and agents of greed,
Its lobbyists and its apologists,
Its copywriters and its journalists,
However elegantly suited,
However suitably elocuted,
And all its supporting professionals,
Its accountants and its solicitors,
Its politicians, even ministers.

Third, I do now heartily deplore
The displacements and distractions
Of space exploration, empty project.
Yes I agree, it's incredible, nearly,
How we know more about Mars' surface

Than how our body works, our brain,
Which can be left to the food industry
And the pharmaceutical industry,
Space so sexy, humanity so boring.

And I will also heartily despise
These recent gleeful pop evolutionists
Who invoke Darwin in order to promote
Their own reductive view of human kind,
Their own self-serving models of selfishness,
Their own closed circles of catch, kill, consume,
And now their insistence that empathy
Is nothing but delusion they can see through.

And so I resolve,
Here before friends and witnesses,
To uphold the civic, the human, and the good,
And everywhere he shows his ugly maw
Throw Mammon and his cohorts out the door.

Winter Spell

Winter trees silhouetted
Along the curve of the hill
Spell something very powerful
Though indecipherable.

Transcendental alphabet
Abstract poems against the light
Shout silently their meaning
Black ciphers against the white.

Simplicity

The plainest of food spiced by hunger
And water made nectar by need
Are better than any rich banquet
However the gastronome plead.

Capital

Received economic opinion says
That London is the main generator
Of wealth, even work, that benefits us all
So don't be a success denigrator.

You don't like our skyline and what it stands for?
It's just a self-confident world city,
The envy of many-some would say all.
Steel and glass isn't going to be pretty.

So all right St Paul's is a little bit lost
Down below amongst skyscraper shadows.
Building always means winners and losers.
Ignore all those nostalgic saddos.

You say there are oligarchs hiding their loot
Helped by lawyers, banks and their cronies?
You'll quickly discover the law's on our side
And that all of your charges are phoney.

Less of a dynamo, more of a cancer?
Now you have taken leave of your senses.
Get out of town by the shortest of routes
Before you commit more offences.

Yes crawl back to your shires and grim northern towns
You sad chavs who share this gross view
And patiently wait for the wealth to seep down.
Hee haw ho! What prize chumps! Toodle oo!

Advent

The start of winter thirty years ago.
Spirals of laurel in the darkened hall
Centring a lighted candle.

Round the circle at intervals
The children wait with theirs unlit.

Advent ceremony begins
And one by one in turn
Each child moves to the centre

Returning with lit candle
Till the circle is complete.

Lights encircling Light
A moment out of time.
The children's faces radiant.

Light for the dark,
Heat for the cold.
The power of this simplicity.

Mill Island

Fair, red-haired ferrywoman Ceri
Drew me across to the island
And the welcoming jetty of Mill House
Hanging improbably over the weir.

The world and most of its burdens
Put aside for this one afternoon
Of watery enchantment midstream
For all of these families and friends.

Neverending the roar of the river
Upended at the ramp of the weir
And still in the midst of the movement
The curl of the standing wave at its base.

Then, asleep, all our dreams and our nightmares
Are ground out to fineness and lightness
To carry away in the morning
Gift of the generous river.

Easy to be present in the present there
Yesterday in Fladbury, Worcestershire.

Leaves from my Diary

I glanced across at the captain
A steely glint in his eye
"Stand by to repel boarders!" he barked
And we all waved our cutlasses high.

Though almost too modest to tell you
I did play a prominent part
Despatching a score of the villains
And removing the pirate chief's heart.

On another occasion the leader
Who liked to ask my advice
On our expedition to climb Everest
Begged me to climb the hard ice.

"Will it go, do you think?" he pleaded.
"Should be a doddle," I said
So I lugged him up to the summit
But gave him the credit instead.

On Wednesday I swaggered down Main Street
With the leather tough Kid by my side
Lookin' for a gang of bandidos -
With the Kid there ain't no place to hide.

De saloon was de place where we found 'em
"I'll take de big guy" I said.
Out came de hardware on both sides.
In a minute we'd filled 'em with lead.

Finding myself in Milano
On Thursday passing La Scala
I practised my fine tenor voice
With my own composition - an aria.

Hearing my voice the director
Insisted the star move aside
For me to perform-per favore-
The audience bravo'd and they cried.

On Friday they begged for assistance
With skippering the America's Cup
So I slipped on my oilskin one-piece,
Assured them their asses I'd whup.

The gale-force winds just suited us,
We flew to the first marker buoy.
The might of America left floundering
As we wrenched back the Cup - pure joy!

On Saturday no time for adventure
When the alarm clock went off at eight,
I'd been told by my wife we were shopping
And, er, she ticks me off if I'm late.

Aneto, Pyrenees

Leaving the Refugio Renclusa by headtorch
We climbed up Maladetta's flank
To reach the ridge's higher gap,
The Portillon Superior,
And so descend to the glacier
Onto which we gingerly stepped,
New crampons biting and yard-long axe,
Ash-shafted, accompanying our stride
On the crossing to the summit dome.

Did we put the rope on for the traverse
Of the final airy obstacle,
The Punta de Mahoma, so-called,
Knife blade to Paradise?
I can't remember. This was seventy nine,
And that was forty years ago.
We asked a fellow ascentionist,
A Spaniard, if he'd take our summit snap.
"Con la virgen o no?" he asked.
With the brand new silver-painted virgin
Or not, he wanted to know, offering the choice.
"Yes, chuck her in," we irreverently replied,
"If the price is just the same." And so
We were immortalised, cocky youngsters
Sunlit on Aneto's highest point,
Before the descent to Artiga de Lin,
Its resounding boards,the corner barrel
And that memorably simple meal.

Their dancing child, her beauty, and he
Looking daggers as he grilled the skewered meat.
"Y para postre?" And for our dessert
A whole pear each and perfectly ripe.

A quarter of a century later,
This time not with Brian but Denver,
Staying again at the Renclusa.
But from the Portillon Superior
Stepping onto, what! It's rock not ice,
The glacier retreated
About a quarter of a mile,
The summit virgin black from lightning strikes,
Time and its effects too evident.

I cannot properly believe
That geological events, no less,
Could happen in my lifetime…
No, truly, much less than that.
What melted snows will feed the Aragon,
Feed the Esera valleys and their parched lands
Just a few years hence,
Now that the glaciers are going,
Now that the glaciers are gone.

Inversion

I started in shadow,
Shadow of freezing fog
Isolating everything,
Separate each tree.
The track climbed the hillside
But why should I continue?
The view will be shut off.
Till suddenly just short
Of the escarpment edge
Brightness shone overhead,
The white disc of the sun
In the thinning vapours.
Virtuous work rewarded
I emerge upon the top,
Intense reflected light,
Into a blue hemisphere.
Now below, the level fog
Encircles, and my shadow,
Arms spread wide with wonder,
Is outlined with a rainbow
Across the sea of cloud.
Yes a brocken spectre
First observed and noted
On the Brocken mountain,
Now here on Bredon hill.
I greet other people
Each dazzled by our fortune,
Find reasons to delay.

Then down into the murk
That would last all day,
Transcendence a memory
That would last all year
Now recorded here.

Mockcracy

Yes, be a chum to the scum
So that we can
Bash down better
Crack down harder
Drill down deeper
Smash down smaller.

First give'em the old thumbs up
We're mates, don't ever forget
Then into the dressing-up box.
Plenty of japes and jokes galore
So plenty of photo-ops.

We're levelling up, aren't we Dom? Er, Dom?
We'll build back better, I swear.
We're blaming the E.U. for our Brexit.
Our higher jab rates only fair.

Get that flag on the building, or else.
Brits are best with their backs to the wall
Traitors alone will resist it.
Confrontations? We'll win 'em all!

Get the job done. Do it quickly.
They like to see a bit of speed
Fuck the moaners and their allies,
Fuck the needy, feed the greed.

All right, 'we' means 'I' you've got it,
Don't be a dork it's rhetoric
Biggest joke in the whole circus
Is that they'll still vote for us.

Like to sing it in the shower,
Even when I'm shagging Caz,
Suitable for any hour
Including while I'm having a waz.

(To the tune of the national anthem)

Bash down much better
Drill down much deeper
Seems we just can't fail.
Smash down much smaller
Crack down much harder
Take the knee to your premier,
We, we, we, me, me.

Boriface

Our heroic P.M. went to Eton
Where tradition required you were beaten
And where you were taught
All the others were naught
And the key skills of lyin' and cheatin'.

King of the Shysters

The King of the Shysters, one Trump
On the whole world attempted to dump.
After four years however
He quit the endeavour
When voters kicked him up the rump.

For Ken Dodd

Happiness?
It's behind you!

Traitor?

Why do I now recoil
When I see the union flag
Or worse the flag of St George?
No flag makes my tail wag.

Why do I always resist
Singing God save the Queen,
Or the last night of the proms
With its patriotic songs.

You can choose your poppy red
That glorifies one side
And ignores the enemy dead
And civilians who died.

I need a wider vision
Than narrow nationalism.
I'd salute a flag of the world
If that were instead unfurled

Night Male

This is the nightmare hurtling towards us
Bringing a tyrant to appal us,
Privilege for the rich
Deception for the poor
Haranguing the press
And revoking the law.
Rip up the treaties
Ignore human rights,
Make friends with the vicious,
With allies pick fights.
Facts you deny
And lies you approve
All those damn foreigners?
They've just gotta move.
Climate change denier,
Let's just go for broke.
Stand up and shout it:
Obama was a joke.
Torture is good,
I'll bring it all back
To boss my great country
No weapons I'll lack.

Male, white and loaded
Are the core of his team,
A nightmare for the world
But for him it's a dream.

A nightmare should end
When the sun first appears
On the eastern horizon
But this Monster's for real.

Top Man Tutorials

Introduction: no introduction
Just give 'em the goods.
Numero Uno:
You would not be here
Listening to me
If you did not crave success.
Am I right or am I wrong?
If wrong, save your money
And leave before I start…
OK let him go,
I got nothing to say
To no patsies
To no snowflakes.

So we begin.
Put away those notepads.
This is live, life is live.
Numero Due:
Always but always
Ahead of the curve.
Better, ahead of the curve
That you're slightly ahead of.
You gotta get there first
And they're all running flat out.

Numero Tre: zeitgeist shitegeist.
Tomorrow's too late.
Today is yesterday on the way.
YOU gotta set the zeitgeist.
And keep it simple.
You think we got a multitude
Of genii outside this place?
I don't think so.
Tell em what you're gonna tell em
Then tell em
Then tell em what you told em.
Reinforce the message.
Repeat, repeat, repeat.
I repeat: REPEAT.

Numero Quattro:
Morality got no place here.
Morality's for the multitude,
Keeps em nice and malleable.
Malleable: like you fashion it
Exactly the way you want it.
No right, no wrong.
Just what works.
And it ain't gonna
Work for long
So change it.
Keep it new and fresh.

Numero Cinque:
We love humanity,
Dey're the raw material.
Long as they've got
A purse or a pocketbook.
It is entirely impossible
To overestimate stupidity
So keep it simple.
And what a material to craft
The way you want it.

Numero Sei:
And by the way, never go
Beyond numero sei-
Sell em the dream
But above all
Sell em the brand.
Big, bold, brash, bright.
The golden glow that everybody wants,
The growing dawn of the new day
With your name in the middle.

And when you get to the top
Come and knock on my door.
Success welcomes success
So only the winners.
Show me the second
And I'll show you the first loser.
You got all that?
Right, get out of here
And go go GO for it.

Hunters

Shriek of falcon
Cronking raven
Timid jay upon the ground
Search for food for their survival
To this cycle they are bound.

Jolt of gun on wooded ridges
Violent sport whose aim's to kill
Bloody pheasants by the hundred
Lie about the joyless hill.

Whoa, Man!

Men enjoy bars
Driving fast cars
Declaring wars
Paying for whores
Having no cares
Threatening stares
Answering dares
Throwing downstairs
Ignoring laws
Kicking down doors
Befriending bores
Pointing out flaws
Of disputes the cause
Sharpening their claws
Sinking their pars
Having their jars
Thinking they're stars.
Men are from Mars.

Woman replies
Yeah, whatever…

Harpers Bazaar

I wish to celebrate Harpers Bazaar
A mixture of junk shop and gallery,
A riotous eccentric assortment
Worth more than an oil sheikh's salary.

I know – don't get carried away – it's a shop
And Laurence just making a living
But if you enjoy the oddness of dreams
It's a place that keeps giving and giving.

Need a pith helmet? You're at the right place.
Want to hide? racks of camouflage suits.
Boots for the hills or sledge for the snow,
All the kit for your favourite routes.

Guides and Scouts can be uniformed here,
D of E groups try on their huge rucksacks.
O.K. that cannon was never for sale
But we're all on the look out for knickknacks.

I went in this week and I really must say
That the splendid ceremonial dress
Of the Intelligence Corps, green velvet brocade,
Caught my eye. Must go back and say yes.

Don't tell the P.M. or he'll be along
As his dressing up box is nearly empty.
Hard hats and bibs, aprons, medical kits,
The Bazaar could supply him with plenty.

And so, sad to say, a very farewell
To providers of Malvern Link colour
You've brightened our lives with countless supplies
We cannot expect such another.

Personal Pronouns

Don't include me in your 'We'
It's you and your crew
And it's us you're trying to screw.
'We' tries to divert the blame,
For you a political game
Playing with the pronoun
And acting the clown
For corporate interests to prevail
The only thing that must not fail.

Haiku

Euthanasia?
Offends hypocratic oath -
Just fuck off and die

Ho ho

The inventor of the limerick, Edward Lear,
Wrote many which weren't funny, I fear,
With five lines, so few,
He thought four would do,
The inventor of the limerick, Edward Lear.

Plucky Pensioner (66) Protests Press Prejudice

In an unprecedented protest
Plucky Pensioner Percy Pumpkin (66)
Has challenged news - room policies.

Clearly cloyed by clichéd descriptions
Of people of pensionable age,
Mr Pumpkin (66) has posed the question
'Why mention pensioners in the first place
And why put their age after their names? '

Tired of playing the colourful clown,
Local personality Pumpkin (66)
Asks if an ageist policy
Is permitted, even promoted,
In press-rooms up and down the country

Prejudice against older people
Is prohibited in the Penal Code
And panders to a patronising
Predisposition in most people.

Praise for the important point you raise,
You've posed us a puzzler, Percy (66).

Adventure

Regarding children's personal growth,
An outdoor centre for a week
Is worth a year - maybe much more -
Of normal classroom work.

The residential experience where
You live and eat together
In carefully sorted activity groups
To breakdown school-induced barriers.

And then the range of challenges
With their different kinds of demands
Cave, cliff, mountain, river, the sea,
You'll find at least one of them hard.

Amongst the most telling memories
On the knife-edge ridge, a girl so slight,
Reassuring a strapping youth
Who was gripped and frozen with fright.

And the first taste of sea canoeing
Paddling through a colony of seals
And... what! The arc of bottle-nosed dolphins
Was that a dream or was it real?

In utter dark, exploring caves,
Sounds, colours and scents forsaken.
And now the relief rediscovering the world
As we emerge and our senses reawaken.

Then the mumbling line, slogging up the slope,
And the wait for the panting last person,
But the widening view high above the vale
And the joy of the shared summit moment.

Sometimes a vista shows nothing man-made
Just ourselves and primeval nature
Time itself briefly set on one side
For a taste of being immortal.

Then round the meal table that evening
Excited young voices tell their tale
And no one has time to feel homesick
Experiences that will never go stale.

Inspired by events and the landscape
Some seek expression in music and art
For others it's opened a window
For memories feeding the heart.

Returning just a week later,
Fully exercised mind, body, soul,
And friendships with previous strangers
Scattered fragments now become whole.

Living Link

Plonked as a babe in grandad's lap
Who was born in eighty five
In my lap grandson plonked in turn
Who next century should be alive.

Which would make me, which may make you,
A three century living span,
Carrying the precious charge of life
Through generations.

Alchemy

Never confuse God and Gold
There's an L of a difference.

Society

My right to swing my arm
Ends where your nose begins
And your right to do the same-
So in that way we're twins.

Your child is mine to care
And my own child is yours,
Pole that points our compasses,
Basis of love and laws.

Each new child, we've been told
Offers another chance
For nature to remedy culture's mistake.
Only thus we advance.

Let's take a break

We value your idiocy
In believing our assertion
That we value your privacy.

And yes, I accept all porkies
Because they enhance my experience
Of micro-tailored marketing.

And of course I'm excited
By these 200 mph ads.
Hurtling round the grand prix course.

And the interviews with pro golfers
Half of their faces visible
Beneath the sponsorship contracted cap.

Prominent on the grimmest high streets
The bookies' names on half the chests
Of premiership millionaires.

Yes, mendacity's the theme
And many of our politicians
Would not have it otherwise.

But now we'll take a break
        Got it!

Harder. Better. Stronger. Faster

The face in the rear view
Bearing down on you
Glaring down on you
The intense LED light lines
Above the narrowed eyes
Designed for the expression
Of all too clear aggression.

Or the dazzling circular stare
Saying I want to come through
So, quick, move over you.
Too wide to fit in the lane
But indisputably male
The ones who choose the make
The ones who must not fail

Aloft, so able to look down
From their tank-like S.U.V.
And able to banish for a while
Their status anxiety
That special English affliction
Born of class and the elevation
Of received pronunciation:
Instant and deadly relegation.

Memorial Orchard

At The Woodland's end an open field
Leaning south towards the sun
Is the memorial orchard
Each tree chosen, each tree planted
For a loved person now gone.

Community Woodland, blessed name,
Welcoming green space we can share
And the orchard lines of local trees
And the seasonal waves of wild flowers
Deserve our regular care.

Right at the top of the orchard
A single tree stands above
Crab apple that keeps its fruit into spring
Food for birds when the winter is hard
Apt symbol for motherly love.

Outside the laws of accepted faith
This is one way we still can
Experience what sacred means
Trees and light and paths and memory
And mortality of man.

Touch the screen to start

The sweet-toned Bot gives her order
To touch the screen to start
But unlike the girl at the check-out
A Bot ain't got no heart

I'll always choose a person
Not touch the screen to start
I want to be served by a human
Not told to add to cart.

The customer in front of me
Is having a bit of a chat
With Steph – he even knows her name
I will not blame him for that

I don't want Steph to be replaced
She doesn't just tot up the sums
She'll chat and try to be pleasant
To whoever for her services comes.

It's the things that keep us human
That should be top of the list
It's the bots that are redundant
Rip them out – they will not be missed.

The Bostin Babby Levels Up

We sin it in the Express and Star
An jus noo we'd gorra goo
Me, Micky an Balthazar.
We thought we'd berra tek a prezzie
You know, journeyin from afar,
And wid already ad the first snow

It were a biruvva crazy story
Tharra virgin were avin a babby
That the ole man were an angel
An the babby, the bostinest ever born,
Would be with us with with the new dawn –
Do they think we ain't got no savvy?

Er other ole man were a chippie
You know, an ordinary bloke like us.
O dunno ow'e pur up with it
Irrud mek your average saint cuss
Bur instead they wuz talkin about miracles
Ow the ole thing were miraculous

They wuz roun the back in an out'ouse
In a stall where the osses were kept
A lantern lightin their faces
While the bran new babby slept.
Micky give im a blanket, Bal'e give im a doll,
Me o give im the fossil I'd got workin the quarry spoil.

We soon snuck away after that though
We noo that we'd gorra get back
Wi the picture still bright in our startled bonce
Of all that wid sin and wid done
O'coulda sworn we was floatin' not walkin'
Back'ome to Dudley still on its bonk.

That babby grew up from kiddie to man
An nothin's bin jus the same since
In this ole world o' wenches and blokes
Since God come down to Earth a human
An showed ow the seeds of sacred an 'oly
Are alive in just ordinary folk
Ow we're all of us ordinary folk.

Fencote

Toiling up through late December mud
I discovered this remote surviving station
Atop its long hill since 1888,
Its last passengers to depart seventy years ago
Yes, threescore years and ten, allotted span.

Long closed of course but lovingly maintained:
Its signal box, its waiting room and hearth,
Its ticket office, churns lined on the platform,
Its innocent holiday posters, Ladies and Gents.
You'd swear you heard the sound
            Of the approaching train.

And here they are, the girls in frocks,
            the boys in shorts,
Mothers in their crinolines, men bewhiskered,
As the train exhales and baggage is unloaded.
Then doors are slammed, a green flag waves,
            a whistle blows
And it all begins its squealing steep decent.

Suddenly I'm back with the old family albums,
Blurry sepia to begin with then black and white.
Look here is my grandmother, Cecily Iona Gwynn
Whom I never met, her beauty radiant still,
            neutralising time.
What a story she would surely tell me.

But sadly unrecorded names of great uncles and aunts,
Smudgy and stiff in their formal clothes and groups
At long-forgotten family events.
They were as real as you and I are now,
Properly attentive to their present, their here and now.

So Fencote I must say thank you for the time and place
To bring to you my sepia past
For a meeting on this station platform
Of all these imaged and imagined souls
This my delighted shout of affirmation.

Blind Date

Alexandra   and   Robert
Autovocal Adviser   Alpha Systems Designer

Alexandra, what were you hoping for?
      Buzzy interconnectivity
What were your first impressions?
      His voice was a bit mechanical until
      fully synchronised. His expression
      was a bit blank. Faint internal
      noises.
What did you talk about?
      Everything and everyone, past,
      present and especially future.
Any awkward moments?
      When I popped to the lube for
      a top-up and nearly tripped
      over his cable.
Good table manners?
      I got used to it, but he ate
      with his fingers.
Best thing about Rob?
      When I saw the size of his
      algorithm. Nice gleam and sparkle.
      The occasional flash.
What do you think he made of you?
      He dismantled my left hand
      and made a toy car.

Would you introduce him to your friends?
        Probably, but I was concerned when
        he told me he had an appointment
        at the re-gendering clinic.
Did you go on somewhere?
        Yes, to the Bots Bare-all Ball.
And… Did you kiss?
        I tried but he had no lips.
        This amused me as he had
        started to call me Tulip.
        He asked me to call him Robbo.
If you could change one thing about the evening
what would it be?
        I've been infected with
        malware ever since. I don't
        want to blame Robbo but
        he's just disappeared off the screen.

Marks out of ten?
        Bleep bleep bleep bleep bleep
Would you meet again?
        Maybe somewhere out in
        the Metaverse where my
        thoughts always dwell.

Map Music

Scour the maps I have of the place I live
And all of its roads and its lanes,
Its bridleways, its footpaths and fields
Revealing a treasury of names.

Want a hill to climb? Try Poll Noddy,
A stroll up those Butterley Orles,
Pimple Hill, The Goggin and Bagpipers Tump.
Do you feel the strength of their calls?

Some of the names hint a grim story –
Cut Throat Lane, Kill Horse Lane, there're two,
But we've Nests for Raven, Wren and Martin,
And White Leaved Oak, Gospel Oak, Gospel Yew.

There's Paradise Brook to set against Sodom,
Here are Tumpy Lakes for a swim,
Paradise Green where Hope Springs arise,
Golden Grove we must reverently hymn.

Burley Gate, Englands Gate, bid you enter,
Gobs Castle, The Gobbets, a curious peep,
Pudleston, Bockleton, Crumplebury Farm,
Ham Bridge and Pie Corner to eat.

But do not omit the prosaic –
We know where we stand in Five Acre Wood,
Bull Field just sounds its own warning,
Green Lane still beckons as it should.

Gruesome steep dingles sometimes abound
Within a few miles opening forth.
Witchery Hole, Hell Hole, Devils Den,
Death's Dingle itself staring north.

Amongst them ascending a pilgrimage route
To the Holy spring leads a way
For legions and travellers and faithful,
Still sweet-tasting water today.

At the end of these searches the Poets Stone stands
Next to Sunny Bank Dingle in these folded lands
And this paper map breathes many mysteries to me
Alive with its names as any story can be.

Cairn

Mountain summit cairn
Secular shrine
Made by hundreds of hands
With the stone that you found
Amongst all the rest.
A tapering structure
That points at the sky,
Horizon encircling
Where earth and air touch.

Distractions down below,
Present here in the present.
Someone once said
That God is a circle
Whose centre is everywhere
And circumference is nowhere.
Another advised
Lift the stone and you will
Find him. Split the wood
And he is there.

Please grant me at least
That after the climb
Our soul seeks a harbour
To unburden our freight
And complete this strange voyage.
So, refreshed and restored,
The cairn now grown slightly,
We begin the descent
To the world down below
Our spirit still aglow.

Domes De Miage, Chamonix

Just a night and day
Thirty odd years ago
The hut was full so we slept outside.
Then out of our bivi bags
And gear up in the dark
Head torches searching the route
And onto the glacier.

An early hours start
Is the only way
To ensure the snow bridges
Across the crevasses
Are solid to bear our weight.
With the rope taught between us
As we grope our way up.
Still dark when we emerge
From the maze of the glacier
And start up the snow slope
For the sharp ridge.

It's my first alpine climb
We're moving cautiously
Which means we've been slow
And the dawn is arriving
As we balance up the knife edge
Bound for the top.

Reach the summit by dawn
The mantra that pushes us along
So that the snow is still solid
When on tired legs we descend.
But it's already soft
On the ridge to the peaks
Of the Domes De Miage.

The northeast to our right
Is awash with bright colours
While night remains still
On the glacier we climbed.

Now the shared summit moment
Permits us a pause
But we must not delay.
The descent begins slushy
And soon we are wallowing
Up to our knees then
Taking a slide and a tumble
Beneath the hot sun.

At last we're on rock
The track goes past the refuge
And down to the road and valley
And its offerings of green for the eye
Food and drink for the body.

Now sitting outside in the light
Still buzzing with what we have done

Only one night and a day
And that half a lifetime away.
But see how the memory has stayed
How such a memory can't fade

A Liddle Local Difference

On de mean streets of Ledbury
Der is one block
Between 15th and Mabel's Orchard
You don't wanna look.
Der's a hangout called Oice Boites
-What kinda Name's dat?-
Where de Shoiks and de Jets
Toit dey'd go nap.
I ain't toikin' cards
I'm toikin' turf wars:
For controil of de territory
Out came de boys.

Ledbury's a town
Where you don't wanna mess.
Der law, it ain't stoopid,
Dey've just left it, I guess
To shake itself down
Den dey'll clean up de cess.
Now in Ledbury Town
Poetry's big-an I mean BIG-
An' to shift all de shit
You need a good gig.
Most of de noice guys
Dey've ended up dead
Trundlin' in concrete
Tru de banks of de Led.
So we're toikin real serious,
Let's get dis straight'
De Shoiks an der famblies
Got it all on a plate.

Widdout dey say yes
Der ain't nothin' moves-
Der teacake franchise
Is just one of der grooves.
No cake moves an inch
Widdout dey say so
But if you,re a good boy
You can share in de dough.
Mrs Muffin's in Choich Lane's
Der washroom all right
Where dey launder de money
To whitest of white.

Free-range butchery's anudder
Where dey got control,
Ain't a poik chop dat's eaten
Dat ain't paid de toll.
But butchers an' teashops
Dat's jus' chicken feed stuff,
Poetry's mainline,
Dey jus' can't get enough.
So jus' like de teacakes
An' jus' like the chops
When it comes to de pomes
-an' I mean de whole shebang:
Production, Distribution,
Protection. Remooneration-
When it comes to de pomes
It's de shoiks call de shots.

But onto dis happy scene
Der falls a shadow,
A noo bunch o' guys
Are up in the saddle.
Dey call themselves Jets
An' dey're lookin' for land
Deir biros an' pens
Dey are hot in deir hand.

For a coupla weeks
It was evens, dey say,
Some deaths on each side
Other lives'd have to pay
-Also a whole lotta collateral damage-
Things weren't goin'nowhere
Till a shoik had a thought
-An' it ain't every day
A Shoik manages a whole thought
All on his own-
"We could save on de bloodshed
If just two of us fought."
De noos it spread fast
Dat a dool ud take place
Wid de boss of de Shoiks
And de Jets face to face.

Nick opened proceedins
With a well-crafted line.
It smacked Dan in the midriff
But he said he was fine.
Danny swung a couplet
That caught Nicky's head, He rocked for a moment.
What's in that glove? Lead?
Nick socked him a sonnet,
All fourteen lines.
Dan swayed an' his eyes glazed,
But he held on in time.
Back came a haiku,
Dat's five-seven-five,
An old eastern trick,
But,hey!we're still alive.
Quick as a flash
With an Auden quotation
Nick got in a body blow
Which drew admiration.
Danny countered with a limerick,
A doity one at that.
Nick doubled in laughter,
His knees hit the mat.
But he's back on his feet.
At the end of the round
Danny's come out de worse.
Nick thinks he smells blood
An' moves in for the kill,
A chunk of free verse
Should just fit de bill.

You can see Danny's hurt
By the look on his face.
But whateva is dis?
His wig's slipped its place.
At last all stands clear
Dan is not one of us,
He's flutterin' his eyelids
An' dat chest is a bust.
It's now clear he's a broad
Dressed up as a guy,
An' to make matters worse
Now she's startin' to cry.
Finish her, Nick!
Was the shout from his gang,
But Nick is a gent
An' lets his gloves hang.
Daniella looks up
An' sees her big chance:
Astounding alliteration,
Astonishing assonance.
Nick folds to de canvas
An' measures hi length.
De Jets' super-hero
Has been sapped of his strength
By dis fickle Delilah
Who gets de Shoiks' cheers.
From de open-mouthed Jets
It's half-heated jeers.

De ref is bewildered
He looks in de rules
But der ain't one to cover
Broads fightin' dools.
He calls dem together
An' says it's a draw.
Nick, he don't like it
But he offers a paw.
Daniella accepts it
An' flutters her peepers.
Nick's lookin' strange-
O my God, jeepers creepers
What's goin' on here?
Don't fall for her kid!
Dis story's turned puky
So I'll screw down de lid.

De Shoiks an' de Jets
Called a truce de next day
-On a temporary basis, you understand-
An' de Scribes an' de Poets
Joined in de melee.
When dey troo down der arms
What a sight to behold:
sharpened pencils
chewed-down ball-points
front-loadin' propellin' pencils
fountain pens wid rusty nibs
any number o' keyboards
a typewriter and
one packet o' fluorescent glitter gel pens.

An' de paper!
Spiral bounds, jotters,
Post-it notes, writing pads,
An' note pads of every size an' color
A4 sheets wid an'widdout margins,
Even ol'envelopes an' table napkins.

-A truly sickenin' sight
Which struck dumb de townsfolk
Whose hearts dey jus' froze
Dat all dis sick scribblin'
Was jus'under der nose.

Now I'm sure dat you know dis
But under der armour
All hoods an' gangsters
Dey luvva der mamma.
Show me a gang boss
Or show me some muscle,
Der hearts are marshmallow
When dey ain't on de hustle.
So wid Christmas approachin'
-Am I really sayin' dis?-
It's hugs an' embraces
An' a big sloppy kiss.

De vendetta's over
De moral now comes:
Put de hardware away
An' stick to de pomes.

Golden Valley

Surrealism doff your cap
At Kilpeck Church in Herefordshire
Its corbel dreams and nightmares
Still sharp in stone nine hundred years.

Nearby the River Dore descends
Down the vale of enchantments
Wide-open limbs enclosing all
Its secrets and excitements.

A Marches blend of cultures here
Where Wales and England blur
Among these convoluted flanks
And along the golden floor.

Alice walked this wonderland,
Aslan lost his life up here,
Fictions of Carroll and Lewis
Who both held this valley dear.

So much here to draw the eye
Still quiet its narrow steep lanes
Calls to adventure everywhere
Wells, castles, churches, remains.

Somehow not surprising therefore
In Dore Abbey a voice of beauty
Singing sacred songs to the East,
Performing her Easter duty.

Peterchurch symbol is a fish
Round its neck a chain of gold
Brought for the monk who sought it.
Down in Dore's waters cold.

Golden some say with buttercups, daffodils,
With wheat some others prefer,
The river has it for its name
And Welsh for water is Dwr.

Walk by the disused railway line
Visit the twelfth century inn
Sip clean water from one of its wells
Wherever you choose is a win.

Lewis thought it a vision of heaven
Heart-churning beauty sublime
This song of praise I am singing
To step for a while out of time.

Index of first lines